SHARKS

NICK ARNOLD

ILLUSTRATED BY DAVE SMITH

www.horrible-science.co.uk

Visit Nick Arnold at
www.nickarnold-website.com

Scholastic Children's Books,
Euston House, 24 Eversholt Street,
London, NW1 1DB, UK

A division of Scholastic Ltd
London ~ New York ~ Toronto ~ Sydney ~ Auckland
Mexico City ~ New Delhi ~ Hong Kong

First published in the UK by Scholastic Ltd, 2011

ISBN 978 1407 11106 3

Printed and bound by Tien Wah Press Pte. Ltd, Singapore

2 4 6 8 10 9 7 5 3 1

CONTENTS

. . . .

INTRODUCTION

So you want to be a shark-spotter?

What, *really?*

Wouldn't you be a teeny bit terrified if you had to swim with a man-eating shark? This man is. Meet Harvey Tucker, Australia's biggest journalist (and let me tell you, he's a lot larger than the others).

Harvey used to write articles for *Living on the Edge* magazine about how he wrestled crocodiles and skydived over Mount Everest.

Then the editor found out that the nearest Harvey gets to danger is watching extreme sports on TV whilst guzzling a giant bag of popcorn. Now Harvey's got one last chance to prove he's a genuine action hero...

The editor wants an article. And this time Harvey's got to write about how he swam with a great white – the biggest hungriest man-eating shark in the ocean! Will Harvey end up with all his arms and legs? Well, why not dive into this book and find out? By the end you'll be a fully trained shark-spotter, and you'll know whether sharks really deserve their bad name.

Ready to take the plunge?

SAVAGE SHARK ATTACKS

Harvey Tucker, the greediest journalist in Australia, has been ordered to swim with a great white shark. Right now, he's poring over a pile of shark attack stories whilst snacking on a jumbo-sized packet of crisps. Want a peek?

PACIFIC NEWS
July 1945
SHIPWRECKED SAILORS IN SHARK SNACK SHOCK!
At least 100 US sailors have been snapped up by sharks after a Japanese sub sank their battleship. The suffering sailors, many injured, were dragged to their doom by the savage sharks in three days and nights of awful attacks. Said one survivor: "I thought I was a hard-bitten seafarer but I'm a bit more bitten now!"

AUSTRALIAN NEWS

December 1963

SAVAGE SHARK BITES FOX

Spear-fishing champ Rodney Fox is the latest dauntless diver to fall victim to the great white shark. Rod was set to win the Australian Spearfishing Championships when the marine monster grabbed him. Fearless Fox fought back, catching his hand in the shark's giant jaws. As he surfaced, the savage shark came back for a second helping.

Battling Rodney kicked the creature, but it ate his float, dragging him down with it. Luckily, just before he drowned, the float line broke. Fortunate Fox surfaced near a rescue boat – but if the chewed-up champ hadn't been wearing a wetsuit, his guts would have spilled out. It took 360 stitches to stick the shattered spearfisherman back together. But he's lucky – he lived to tell the tale.

Many shark victims only escape by fighting off their attacker. Twenty years before Rodney Fox's close call a man named Hubert Kabat had to battle for his life...

Shark attack report by Lieutenant-Commander Hubert R. Kabat (US Navy) November 1944

After the enemy sank my ship, I was thrown into the water. I felt something scratch my left foot. It was gushing blood and I glimpsed the brown back of a giant shark swimming away. For a second I thought it had gone, but to my terror, it turned and rushed towards me.

I hit the shark, but it tore at my left foot until my big toe was dangling from a strip of flesh, and then it bit off a chunk of my right heel. Then it bit my left elbow. My calf was torn and bleeding. I knew I would die...

Then I saw a ship. I waved my arms, I yelled. The sailors fired at the shark. Bullets zipped into the water all around me, and I was scared that I'd be shot. I pleaded with them to stop. After I was pulled from the sea, I noticed that my injuries hadn't hurt. Had I been too shocked to feel them?

I could tell you hundreds more true stomach-turning shark stories but they're all strangely similar. An innocent human is grabbed by a savage shark and later a leg gets washed up on a beach. So instead here's a queasy quiz. As a budding shark-spotter, can you tell a terribly true tale from a fishy fable?

SHARK-SPOTTERS' TRAINING TEST: SPOT THE TERRIBLY TRUE TALE

TRUE/FALSE

1 In 1935 cops found a murdered gangster's arm in a shark's stomach.

2 When a famous explorer met a great white shark, the toothy terror pooed and fled in fear of the human!

3 In 1972 a shark was served at a Hong Kong restaurant. It proved to have a man's head in its mouth.

4 In 2008 a boy was bitten by a shark ... in his own bedroom!

5 In 2007 a British angler was eaten by a shark he had just caught.

PHY 2PL

Answers:

TRUE TALES

1 You can find this story in most shark books. It happened in Australia – but although a man stood trial for the murder, there wasn't enough proof to convict him. I guess the shark meant the gangster no 'arm.

2 Explorer Jacques Yves-Cousteau (1910–1997) swore it was true.

4 Sort of. It was actually a set of shark jaws and the boy was sleepwalking.

FISHY FABLES

3 As far as I know.

5 The shark (a small dogfish), nipped the angler's nose whilst passers-by pointed and laughed.

All those shark stories have left Harvey Tucker feeling as wobbly as a jellyfish and as green as a parrotfish. So, just for Harvey, here are a few facts designed to show why we shouldn't be so scared of sharks.

REASONS WHY YOU PROBABLY WON'T GET SCRUNCHED BY A SHARK NEXT TIME YOU GO FOR A DIP

1 Shark attacks are incredibly rare. Millions of us swim in the sea, but only about 100 people get attacked and fewer than 30 get killed each year.

2 Shark experts think you've got more chance of being hurt by...

BONK

A COCONUT FALLING ON YOUR HEAD

P-ZZZZAPP

BEING STRUCK BY LIGHTNING

A COLLAPSING TOILET

A VICIOUS HAMSTER

(If you're *really* unlucky, you might be struck by lightning on the toilet, or brained by a coconut chucked by a horrible hamster.)

I'LL TAKE MY CHANCES WITH THE HAMSTER!

3 Most types of shark are less than one metre long and never attack people (you can discover the most dangerous types of shark on page 40).

DO GOLDFISH COUNT AS SHARKS?

But chatting about shark attacks raises a toothy teaser of a question. Why do sharks attack us? As a shark-spotter, you'll really want to know the answer but if you ask a scientist, you'll get three answers (at least).

THEY MISTAKE US FOR ANIMALS THEY EAT SUCH AS FISH OR SEALS.

THEY'RE JUST DEFENDING THEMSELVES – SOME IDIOTS TRY TO RIDE ON THEIR BACKS.

OR THEY HAPPEN TO BE HUNGRY.

Oh dear, I don't give much for Harvey's chances if the great white is peckish. Right now he's trying to get the inside story of sharks and it doesn't smell too good...

SQUISHY SHARK INSIDES

Harvey Tucker has decided to ask the magazine's science reporter, Sally Smart, for help.

Sally makes a call and a few hours later they meet Captain Red Snapper, shark expert and diver, who explains the sort of no-brainer basics that every shark-spotter needs to know before they're allowed to get their feet wet...

SHARK-SPOTTERS' LESSON 1:
SHARK BASICS

Here's a typical shark...

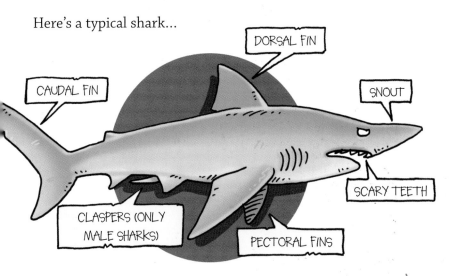

Length: 16 cm to 15 metres depending on species*
Lives: Sharks lurk in most oceans and seas – some species prefer cooler water and some like it warm. No shark spends its whole life in fresh water.
Places to look: Sharks often pop up close to land, hunting for their favourite food – fish and squid. Some sharks prefer the open ocean and others hang out in warmer, shallower water such as the places you might like to swim. Oh dear.

*Species = type of animal. For example, a great white is a species of shark.

Captain Snapper is showing Harvey his favourite shark trophy – Dennis the half-shark. He's trying to explain the difference between a shark and an ordinary fish.

The first thing you need to know is that a shark IS a fish – but it's a very special kind of fish. Just look at the differences between Dennis and Bubbles...

1 Bubbles is covered in slimy scales. Dennis is covered in denticles – they're a bit like tiny teeth.

2 Dennis and Bubbles breathe oxygen taken from the water by their gills. Bubbles' gill flaps waft the water over her gills. Dennis has open gill slits and needs to keep moving to keep the water flowing over his gills. (Most other shark species can waft water over their gills using a small opening just behind their eye.)

If we take a peek inside the two fish, we can see more differences...

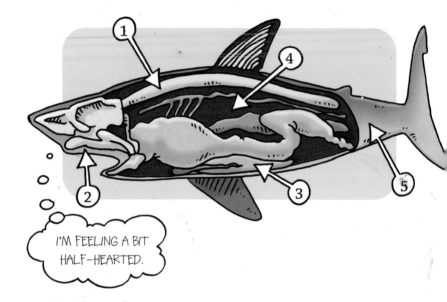

I'M FEELING A BIT HALF-HEARTED.

1 Unlike Bubbles, Dennis doesn't have a bony skeleton. His "bones" are made of **cartilage**, the same rubbery stuff that holds up your ears and nose and cushions the ends of your bones. This makes Dennis's "skeleton" light and bendy and ideal for swimming.

2 Unlike an ordinary fish, Dennis's **teeth** are set in his flesh rather than his jaw. Each tooth grows in a sort of conveyer belt and when it gets knocked out there's always another ready to take its place.

DON'T WORRY READERS, IT'S AN X-RAY. NO GOLDFISH WAS HARMED DURING THE MAKING OF THIS BOOK.

3 Bubbles has a sort of gas bag called a **swim bladder** to make her buoyant (able to float in the water). Dennis has a big oily **liver** to do this job. The liver is lighter than water and Dennis would be sunk without it.

4 Unlike most fish, Dennis has plenty of **red muscle** under his skin. These mighty muscles are for everyday swimming and there's a special blood supply to ensure that heat from the muscles warms the rest of his body. This helps Dennis to live in cold water.

5 It also means the super-powerful **white muscles** he uses for chasing his victims are always warmed-up for action.

Bet you never knew!

1 Fish probably don't burp. But sharks are less shy. As you'll find out on page 72, sharks aren't known for their table manners and if they get gas in their guts they just let out a huge hearty burp.

2 Fish and sharks don't seem to fart, although scientists believe that herring let out gas bubbles to communicate with each other. Next time you make a bottom burp in a swimming pool you could blame it on a passing herring and claim it was a top-secret signal.

But talking about swimming, shark-spotters need to know that there's no substitute for watching a real shark swim and finding out how it uses its fins and tail. Sally and Red are trying to talk Harvey into taking a little swim with the Captain's pet lemon shark...

HARVEY TUCKER IN ... SHORT SHARK SHOCK!

Oh dear, it looks like Captain Snapper doesn't believe in Health and Safety. So is Harvey a lemon's lunch? I'll tell you in a moment...

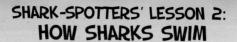

SHARK-SPOTTERS' LESSON 2:
HOW SHARKS SWIM

Think about how you swim – or how Harvey did just now.
We humans push water aside with our arms and legs. This
is hard work – water is 800 times thicker than air, and that's
why you soon get tired when you're swimming. Unlike your
body, a shark's shape is ideal for swimming.

POINTED SNOUT
PUSHES EASILY
THROUGH WATER

ROUGH DENTICLES TRAP WATER
CLOSE TO THE SHARK, ALLOWING
THE FISH TO SLIP THROUGH THE
SEA WITHOUT FRICTION

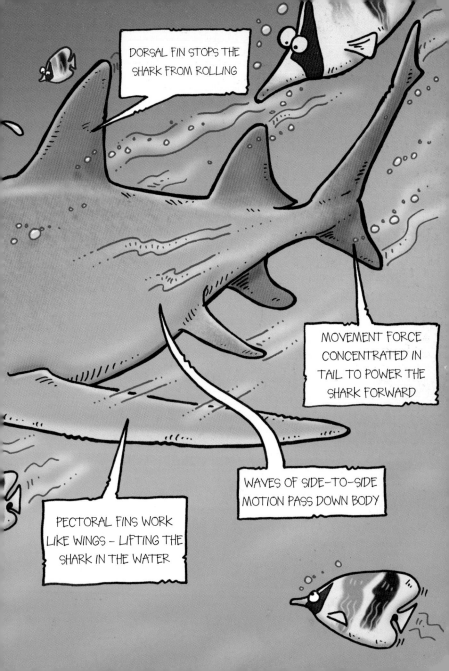

So sharks are champion swimmers – but are they better than us? What do you think?

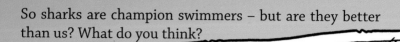

Grand Horrible Science Swimming Gala

Sharks v Humans (the losers get eaten!)

Round 1: Speed

The fastest human can swim at about 8 km per hour.
A blue shark can hit 69 km per hour, a black-tip reef shark can swim at 29 km per hour and a great white can chase you at 25 km per hour.

ROUND 1 TO THE SHARKS!

THE SHARKS

Round 2: Endurance

Slovenian swimming champ Martin Strel enjoys swimming the length of rivers. In 2001 he swam 504 km without a break.
From 1952 to 1956 a grey nurse shark named Skipper swam 168,000 km non-stop in an Australian zoo. (If she hadn't been killed by a porcupine fish she'd have swam even further.)

ROUND 2 TO THE SHARKS!

THE SHARKS

Round 3: Leaping from the water

Great whites do this and mako sharks can leap at 35 km per hour.
(The humans have given up and gone into hiding.)

Well, it's not too shocking that the sharks won the contest – after all, swimming is what they do all the time. What makes them really scary is that their senses are designed for one thing – seeking out flesh to devour. Let's take another peek at Dennis the half-shark...

SHARK-SPOTTERS' LESSON 3:
MAKING SENSE OF SHARK SENSES

A shark is really a finny machine for finding prey (that's what scientists call the creatures sharks eat). And shark senses are the secret to their success...

AM I A HAS-BEEN? OR A HALF-HAS-BEEN?

1 Lateral line contains sensors for detecting movement in water.

2 Bet you never knew that Dennis has ears. They're especially good at hearing underwater sounds, like flapping fish (or human hands and feet).

3 Dennis has taste buds in his giant gob. That's why sharks bite you to find out if you're edible. Why don't they ask politely? That's what I want to know!

4 Electro-detectors on Dennis's snout sense muscle movement in living prey. They detect your heartbeat and can even tell when it speeds up because you're just about to get gnashed. Star shark-spotters call these shocking sensors by their proper name – ampullae (am-pu-lee) of Lorenzini.

5 Dennis can see in colour and make out shades of grey in dark murky water. A shiny layer inside his eyeballs reflects light onto light-sensitive retinas to boost his vision in the dark. Cats use a similar trick. Just like a cat, if you photograph a shark in the dark, its eyes seem to glow. Spooky!

6 Dennis's sharpest sense is his sinister sense of smell. It's especially good at sniffing blood or fish juices in the water.

7 A large part of Dennis's brain is used to detect supper scents.

So how good is a shark's sense of smell? Well, you could try tempting one with your brother's cheesy socks (or even your brother) but here's an alternative that's kinder to sharks.

SHARK-SPOTTERS' TRAINING SESSION:
THE SHARK-SNIFFER BLOOD TEST

You will need:
Some blood (on second thoughts it's better to use red food colouring)
Drinking straw
Spoon
Washbasin
Measuring jug

HORRIBLE FAMILY WARNING
Food colouring can stain your clothes. Wear old clothes for this experiment and take care. You wouldn't want a nasty stain on your character, would you?

What you do:
1 Pour 500 ml of water into the washbasin. Ooops – don't forget to put the plug in first!
2 Now place one end of the straw in the food colouring and pinch the other end. You can use the straw to pick up a drop of food colouring and drip it into the water. Stir the water to mix in the colouring.

3 You should still be able to see a pale pink colour in the water. If this was blood a shark could easily sniff it.
4 Turn on the tap and slowly add water until you can no longer see any colour.

You should find:
By the time the washbasin is full the colour will have disappeared – but of course the colour chemicals are still there. A shark can detect one drop of fish oil in a swimming pool of water.

We can't escape and there's no hiding from them. No wonder people are scared of sharks. Harvey is so scared after his encounter with the lemon shark that he faints. Sally has to revive him with an enormous hamburger.

As a trainee shark-spotter, I bet you're made of tougher stuff. Tough enough to tackle this test, for example...

SHARK-SPOTTERS' TRAINING TEST:
COULD YOU BE A SHARK SCIENTIST?

1 What happened when a Victorian scientist blocked one of a shark's nostrils?
a) The shark snored in its sleep.
b) The shark swam in circles.

2 How did shark expert John McCosker manage to take a great white shark's stomach temperature in 1985?
a) He bravely stuck a thermometer in the shark's bottom.
b) The shark ate the thermometer in a dead tuna fish.

3 Scientists have studied which tastes sharks dislike. What's their *least* favourite?
a) Sea cucumbers
b) Spinach

Answers:

1 b) The shark could only follow scent from one side. The answer couldn't have been **a)** because sharks don't go to sleep.

2 b) The scientist wanted to know how warm the shark's stomach juices were. Warmer juices mean that the shark digests food faster and needs more food. In fact the juices were 6.7°C warmer than the sea. The thermometer was pooed out by the shark.

3 a) Sharks spit them out. Interestingly some humans relish the beche-de-mer sea cucumber in oriental soups.

So how did you get on? Well, if you scored full marks you might think you know all about sharks. Think again! Sharks come in all shapes and sizes including some you won't believe. And if you don't believe me, that's all the more reason to read on!

STRANGE SHARK TYPES

Harvey is back to his old self. In fact, there's even more of his self than there was before, because he's guzzled five hamburgers, three catering packs of cheesy nibbles and a family tub of ice cream.

And now he's feeling brave enough to find out about some strange and savage sharks…

SHARK-SPOTTERS' LESSON 4:
THE VICIOUS VARIETY OF SHARKS

Shark experts reckon that there are at least 400 shark species, but some are very rare, and one is only known because it turned up in the stomach of another shark. The experts divide the species into larger groups called orders – but they're nothing to do with postal orders, doctor's orders, or the sort of orders your parents give you at bedtime.

SHARK ORDERS

SIX- AND SEVEN-GILLED SHARKS AND FRILLED SHARKS

DOGFISH

ANGEL SHARKS

SAW SHARKS

The orders are split into 30 groups called "families", although these aren't the sort of families you'd like to share a toothbrush with. In fact, if you found a shark family in your bathroom, you might like to take a long holiday on Pluto. Fortunately in this book you won't need to worry about which family a shark belongs to. The main thing to remember is that a shark can either be:

If you're a novice shark-spotter, you might be ever so slightly gobsmacked to read that not all sharks like to whizz around scrunching petrified prey. Some squat on the seabed and wait for their prey to drop by for lunch...

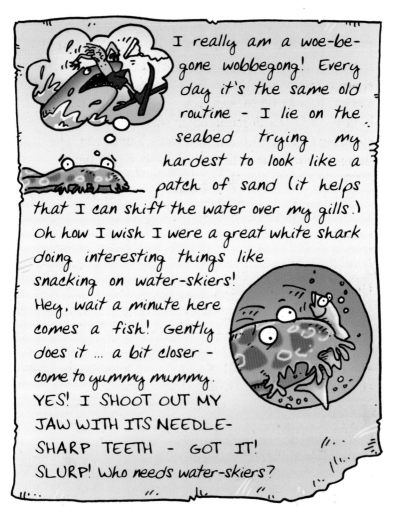

I really am a woe-be-gone wobbegong! Every day it's the same old routine - I lie on the seabed trying my hardest to look like a patch of sand (it helps that I can shift the water over my gills.) Oh how I wish I were a great white shark doing interesting things like snacking on water-skiers! Hey, wait a minute here comes a fish! Gently does it ... a bit closer - come to yummy mummy. YES! I SHOOT OUT MY JAW WITH ITS NEEDLE-SHARP TEETH - GOT IT! SLURP! Who needs water-skiers?

Wobegongs and the other bottom-dwelling sharks aren't exactly dangerous although they might give you a nasty nip if you trod on one. No, the shark species that shark-spotters have nightmares about are the murderous man-eaters...

SHARK-SPOTTERS' GUIDE TO DEEPLY DEADLY SHARKS

Name: **Bull shark**
Size: Males up to 2.1 metres long — females can be 4 metres.
Lives: Close to coasts in warmer parts of the world from California to Australia. They swim up rivers and one was even spotted 4,000 km up the River Amazon. Their bodies take in a lot of fresh water so they have to pee a lot in rivers, and that's one of their nicer habits.

Spotters' note: The horrible habits of the brutal bull shark include hanging around the Ganges Delta, India, and scoffing partly burnt dead bodies that are tipped into the water. It varies its dreadful diet with the live bodies of people bathing.

Danger rating: Get out of the water! The bull shark has killed more than 20 known victims but more are suspected. According to one victim, getting attacked feels like being hit by a truck. But probably a lot less fun.

Name: **Tiger shark**
Size: 3.25—4.25 metres
Lives: Cooler and tropical seas,
especially around Pacific islands.
Although it
prefers open
waters it likes
to cruise close
to land to grab
a tasty bite.

Spotters' note:
It'll scrunch
anything and
anyone. The
tiger shark
gets its name
because its
youngsters are stripy.
Danger rating: You'll need waterproof
pants if you swim near this one. Avoid it
or say toodle-loo to your fingers.
They've killed at least 28 people.

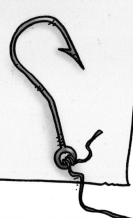

Name: Great white shark
Size: Up to 6 metres, usually 4-5 metres.
Lives: Close to coasts in cooler oceans and the tropics (the warmer parts of the world). It's often spotted off the coasts of California, South Africa and Australia close to islands where seals live. And guess which creatures the sharks like to scoff?

Spotters' note: Some scientists think that great whites don't like the taste of human and only bite us to find out if we taste nice. But you can't have a dainty nibble if your jaws are a cross between a car crusher and a chainsaw.

Danger rating: You'd better leg-it whilst you've still got legs. Great whites have probably killed more humans than any other savage shark species.

You might think that these man-munching, swimmer-scrunching fiendish fish are the last word in sharks but you'd be wrong. The last word in seriously scary sharks was 18 metres long, had 18-cm-long teeth, lived 18 million years ago and fortunately died out 1.5 million years ago. Megaladon was a monster with a bite big enough to swallow a piano (and I bet that would tickle its ivories). Monstrous Megaladon is only known from its terrible teeth. It was once thought to have been the grand-mummy of great whites but now it's thought to have been the grand-mummy of mako sharks instead.

Bet you never knew!

Thanks to fossil shark teeth, scientists have traced sharks back 450 million years. In other words, sharks are three times older than dinosaurs and even older than science teachers. In those far-off days there were spiny sharks and freshwater sharks but the basic body plan hasn't altered much. Why change a winning design?

Although the killer sharks are well-known, there are loads of lesser-known weird and wonderful sharks...

SHARK-SPOTTERS' GUIDE TO STRANGE SHARKS

Name: **Whale shark**

Size: Up to 12.2 metres long and weighs up to 13.6 tonnes.

Lives: Warm oceans in open water.

Spotters' note: It's actually the biggest fish in the world — about the size of a school bus. But even more amazingly, apart from the odd tiddler fish, it mainly scoffs

insect-sized creatures called plankton that it sieves from the sea. Its giant gob is huge enough to seat three people in comfort (well, that's if you can feel comfy when you've just been eaten by a shark).

Danger rating: Being eaten isn't very likely. The wimpy whale shark is actually scared of people. Its almost-as-huge relative the basking shark has a similar laid-back lifestyle.

Name: Thresher shark
Size: 3-6.1 metres
Lives: North American and Asian coasts, plus central and western Pacific open surface waters.
Spotters' note: Even a novice shark-spotter can recognize a thresher by its giant tail. The tremendous tail can take up one-third of its length and the talented thresher uses its tail to thwack fish before gobbling them up as dazed dinner.

Danger rating: Rarely attacks people – but it's best to avoid, otherwise you might have a terrible tail to tell.

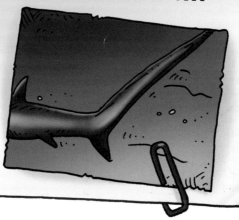

Name: **Hammerhead shark**
Size: 90 cm — 6 metres long
Lives: Warmer seas close to coasts all over the world.
Spotters' note:
No prizes for guessing how this freaky fish got its name.
Scientists think its baffling bonce allows the shark's electrical sensors to scan the sea for prey more effectively. It also has larger nostrils for sniffing out food, and the head works like a wing to lift the shark's front.
Danger rating: Rarely attacks people but shark-spotters should steer clear — you wouldn't want to get hammered would you?

So you think the hammerhead looks like something out of science fiction? Pah – just you wait until you've seen these surprising sharks! Which are real and which are a bit too surprising to be true?

SHARK-SPOTTERS' TRAINING TEST:
SURPRISING SHARKS

TRUE/FALSE

1 The goblin shark is the ugliest shark on Earth. It lives below 200 metres and gobbles squid and deep-sea fish.

2 The megamouth shark uses its giant glow-in-the-dark gulping gob to dispose of jellyfish and plankton.

3 The flower shark got its name from its pretty camouflage pattern.

4 The cookie-cutter shark has the antisocial habit of scooping out bowl-sized bites from other fish. It's even been known to chew a chunk from a passing submarine.

5 The surfing shark often gets a lift over the wave crests. In 1971 one even turned up at a surfing contest, but it didn't win any prizes.

6 With its rather arty bronze colour, the snaggle-tooth shark looks like a 2.4 metre-long goldfish. If you want one as a pet you'll need to feed it squid, crabs and other sharks.

Answers:
Surprising but true **1**, **2**, **4** and **6**.
Surprisingly false **3**, **5**.

But talking about unbelievable sharks, here's a shark that really honestly does exist and it's the fins-down winner of the most unbelievable shark contest…

SHARK SPOTTERS' NEWS
AUG 2004

CRAZY CUDDLES CAUSES CHAOS!

German aquarium owners are shocked by their newest shark. Unlike every other shark in the world, Cuddles is HAIRY, finds her way by touch, and is covered in tiny red plants called algae. Although Cuddles filters plankton she'll scoff anything – including other shark's eggs. Said one baffled boffin: "We don't even know what part of the world she comes from. If I scratched my head much harder I'd get through to my brain!"

But talking about chaos, you'll find a lot more of it in the next chapter. Harvey, Sally and Captain Snapper are about to set sail in search of sharks. And they're sure to find themselves in deep water!

SCARY SHARK SEAS

There's more to shark spotting than spotting sharks. If you really want to know about sharks, you need to know about the creatures that share their sinister sunken world ... Harvey Tucker is about to meet these creatures at Skull Island Reef.*

Hmm – this could get messy – the reef is home to savage sharks. Will the out-sized Aussie suffer grief on the reef with a nasty set of teeth?

We'll come back later when Harvey runs out of excuses... *Five hours later* – ah, at last! Now we can get on with the rest of this book!

*You won't find this place on the map because I've just made it up.

SHARK-SPOTTERS' LESSON 5:
DIVING EQUIPMENT

If you really want to be a fully qualified shark-spotter, sooner or later you're going to have to get in the water with the big biting beasties. And that means learning about diving. Sally has *ordered* Harvey to take a dive. He has two choices of equipment...

OPTION 1 SNORKEL

SNORKEL TUBE TAKES IN AIR FROM SURFACE

MASK HELPS YOU TO SEE UNDERWATER

CAN'T I WEAR ARMOUR?

GLOVES TO PROTECT HANDS

FLIPPERS TO PUSH AWAY WATER AND PROVIDE MORE MOVING POWER FOR SWIMMING

Option 1 is cheap and works well in shallow water. All you do is to lie on your tummy and look down into the water, and hope that an unfriendly seagull doesn't mistake your bottom for a tasty dead porpoise.

But to see more sharks you need to dive deeper, and spend longer underwater. And that's when things get tricky. You see, water is heavy (if you don't believe me try carting around a bucket of the wet stuff). And when you're underwater, the surrounding sea presses on your body and makes it hard to breathe (even if there was any air to gulp). This is called water pressure and it gets worse the deeper you dive.

OPTION 2: SCUBA DIVING

3 COMPRESSED-AIR TANK

HOW ABOUT WATER WINGS?

4 REGULATOR

6 BUOYANCY CONTROL DEVICE

2 WEIGHT BELT

5 DIVE COMPUTER

1 WETSUIT

And here are a few optional extras...

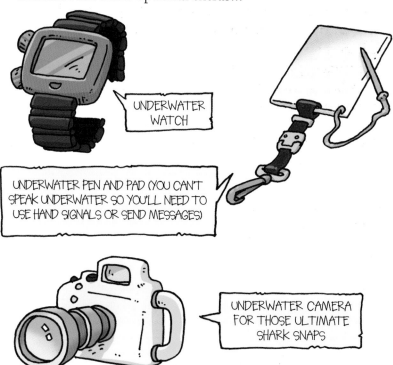

UNDERWATER
WATCH

UNDERWATER PEN AND PAD (YOU CAN'T
SPEAK UNDERWATER SO YOU'LL NEED TO
USE HAND SIGNALS OR SEND MESSAGES)

UNDERWATER CAMERA
FOR THOSE ULTIMATE
SHARK SNAPS

1 The wetsuit is exactly what is says it is on the box. It's a neoprene suit (neoprene is artificial rubber) that lets in a little water. The cold water comes as a shock to shark-spotters, but as the water warms up it works like your very own radiator system.

2 The neoprene contains bubbles, so you need the weight belt to help you sink (the human body floats naturally because it's full of air).

3 Thanks to your air tank, you can stay down for about an hour on a shallow dive.

4 The regulator is crucial to provide air to the diver at the same pressure as the water they're in. This means that the diver's lungs don't get squished.

5 The dive computer tells you how long you can stay underwater – this depends on your depth.

6 But in order to make it back to the surface, you'll need your buoyancy control device (BCD). You fill it with air from your tank and it acts like a life jacket, floating upwards and taking you with it. Well, that's the idea, but when Harvey takes a test dive things don't go to plan...

HARVEY TUCKER IN ... DEEP TROUBLE!

Is Harvey sunk? We'll fish him out later. But talking about fish, let's take a swim around Skull Reef...

WHICH OF THESE CREATURES DID YOU SPOT?

1 Coral – this stuff is made by a creature called a polyp, which is just a few millimetres across. The polyp lives with algae in its own chalky home. Over hundreds of years, the coral builds up to form massive reefs such as the 2,600-km-long Great Barrier Reef. Shark-spotters need to beware of coral – some of it is very sharp and causes nasty infected cuts. Just the sort of grisly gash that sharks like to sniff out.

2 Mackerel – sharks will scrunch any fish that isn't poisonous or prickly. Little sharks scrunch little fish and big sharks prefer whoppers such as tuna and marlin. This mackerel is a favourite fish feast for many sharks. So are herring, whiting, mullet and salmon.

3 Octopus and squid – like many humans, sharks love chewy squid or octopus. Both creatures are molluscs (distantly related to the snails in your garden). But unlike snails, they don't have shells. They have beaks which they use to rip small fish to bits.

4 Crab – these shelly sidelong scuttlers are a favourite shark snack. You can imagine them as shark crisps.

5 Dolphin – sharks can attack dolphins, but not often. Dolphins can attack sharks and beat their insides to goo by ramming them. Mind you, this sort of nastiness is rare – mostly they keep out of each other's way.

6 Turtle – sharks love turtles but turtles aren't turtle-ly fond of sharks.

I could tell you more facts, but right now the fish are fleeing, the turtle is looking terrified and the squid have hid. The most dangerous creatures in the sea are just around the corner. No, they're NOT sharks ... they're humans! Harvey, Red and Sally are looking out for reef sharks to feed with smelly dead fish...

So why did I call the humans "the most dangerous creatures in the sea"? Well, if you were a shark you might well think that. OK, so sharks attack about 100 people a year, but humans slaughter about ONE MILLION sharks for every human victim. Or put it another way, just imagine that sharks scoffed the same weight of humans as we catch of sharks. Within *one year* sharks would have gobbled up every male in Australia.

Many of the bigger sharks are caught for fun by anglers, but sharks do have their uses...

In Sicily they're guzzled with goat's cheese.

In Vietnam it's lime juice, coriander and red-hot chillies.

In the Pacific islands of Melanesia they're roasted on hot rocks and served with coconut sauce.

Either way, the result is the same – the shark gets scoffed. But one revolting recipe is responsible for more slaughtered sharks than any other. I'm talking about traditional Chinese shark-fin soup. Here's how to make it...

Shark-fin soup

Ingredients:
One shark fin (it doesn't matter what shark it comes from)
Stock ingredients (see below)

Method:
1 Remove the skin and meat from the fin. You're left with the cartilage rays that hold it up.

2 Now remove the covering of the rays. The traditional recipe involves boiling the fin every day for five days.

3 Make a tasty chicken stock with mushroom, ham, ginger, onions, soy sauce, rice wine and vinegar. Add salt and sugar to taste.

4 Plop what's left of the fin in the soup.

5 Enjoy!

Actually, many tourists in Hong Kong don't bother to feast on the fin – they prefer to slurp on the soup and leave the fin at the bottom of the bowl. So I guess it's "no fin" to write home about.

Being eaten (or being a leftover) in a soup is bad news for a shark, but it's not the only hazard they face from humans. As you're about to find out, medicine is seriously unhealthy for our finny friends...

• Shark corneas (the front parts of the eyeball) have been transplanted into humans. Well, that will help them see the world through a shark's eyes.

• Shark cartilage has been used to treat burns.

• Shark blood can be used to make substances that stop human blood clotting. Hmm, I guess that blood always flows when sharks are about.

Meanwhile, other industries have also got their beady eyes on sharks...

• Shark oil is used for certain types of makeup.
• Shark stomachs make tasty pet food (tasty if you're a pet, that is).

JAWS

Er, I'm sorry if all that talk about shark stomachs put you off your shark-fin soup, but we really have to return to Skull Island where Harvey's getting wrapped up in his work...

Oh dear – I know I said that sharks eat octopus but there's one octopus that no sensible shark-spotter should tangle with...

Name: **Blue-ringed octopus**
Size: Golf-ball sized.
Lives: Pacific Ocean from Japan to Australia.

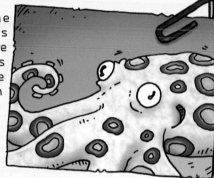

Spotters' note: The odious octopus gets its pretty blue rings when it's angry. Most of the time it blends in with its background until you tread on it. Our intrepid artist has hidden another one somewhere in this book. Can you find it before it finds you? (Answer on page 94.)

Danger rating: The deadly spit stops you moving so that you can't breathe and your heart stops. And there's enough poison to finish off 25 of your friends, too.

And it's at this psychologically challenging moment that the sharks arrive...

SCARY SHARK LIFESTYLES

There's only one thing worse than being stuck with a deadly octopus on your head and a slobbering shark sniffing you out, and that's being stuck in the same situation with TWO slurping sharks. Fortunately, the octopus is as scared of sharks as Harvey and beats a quick retreat, leaving the humans to entertain the sharks. We'll check to see whether Harvey's still got his fingers in a moment. But first a word on safety ... and that word is BEWARE!

SHARK-SPOTTERS' LESSON 6:
SWIMMING SAFELY WITH SHARKS

Swimming with sharks is very silly – in fact, if you happen to be cowardly or sensible you wouldn't do it. But as a seasoned shark-spotter it's part of your job, so you need to know how to do it and come back with all your arms and legs attached.

Shark-spotters safety code

1 *Don't* wear metal. Sharks detect electric currents in metal, remember? Wearing metal attracts them, so leave your chunky, bling jewellery on dry land. Even if the sharks don't attack you, it's bound to offend their fashion sense.

2 *Don't* go swimming at dawn or around dusk. Sharks tend to hunt around these times (and the water is colder at dawn!).

3 *Don't* go swimming with cuts or wounds. They're like a dinner bell to a peckish shark. Peeing in the sea isn't very sensible either – you don't want to give a finny swimmer-snapper the chance to sniff you out.

4 *Don't* go swimming near dead fish for the same reason as in point 3.

5 *Don't* splash the water too much – you'll only draw attention to yourself.

6 *Don't* go alone. Diving is dangerous enough and sharks double the danger.

And talking about a bit of company, sharks rarely go anywhere by themselves. They're a bit like a toothy teacher because they've always got a school with them. A school of fish, that is. But why would any self-respecting fish hang out with a cruel killer?

SHARK-SPOTTERS' GUIDE TO CREATURES THAT SWIM WITH SHARKS

Name: **Pilot fish**
Size: 35—65 cm long
Lives: Warm open seas.
Spotters' notes:
People once
thought that
pilot fish
guided sharks
to food, but
sharks are
smart enough to
find food
without help.
Pilot fish
ride the
underwater

wave produced as the shark swims
through the water. The wave gives the
fish a free ride.

Name: Remora (also known as suckerfish)
Size: 30—90 cm long
Lives: Warm open seas.
Spotters' notes:
Sneaky suckerfish
sometimes stick
their suckers to a
shark and hitch a
free lift. But
mostly they surf
the shark wave.
Each species of
suckerfish
prefers a
different fish
and some suck up
to whales.

Name: Copepods and other pesky parasites
Size: 0.5 mm—20 cm long
Lives: Shark skin and
especially in their
gills.
Spotters' notes:
Parasites feed off
other animals and give
nothing in return.
Sharks have more than
their share of
parasites. Besides
copepods, their guts are
full of tapeworms and
they have leeches living
in their skin and sucking
their blood.

Pilotfish and remoras do sharks a favour by scoffing copepods from their skin and gills and nibbling bits of food from their teeth. It's said that some pilot fish get quite upset when their shark gets caught. Copepods, on the other hand have no redeeming features...

FIVE FOUL COPEPOD FACTS YOU REALLY OUGHT NOT TO SHARE WITH YOUR FAMILY OVER A FISH SUPPER

1 A blue shark can carry up to 3,000 copepods – many in its gills.

2 These delightful beasties slurp the shark's body juices. Some eat dead skin or bury themselves in the shark's flesh.

3 One especially fearless copepod makes itself at home between a great white's teeth. Another snuggles up inside a shark's nostrils.

4 One species of creepy copepod clamps itself to the eyeballs of a Greenland shark, often blinding the unlucky fish. But to be fair, the copepod glows in the dark and may attract prey to the sightless shark.

Back at Skull Island, the sharks prove to be regulars. Captain Snapper has fed them many times before, and you might be surprised to read that they politely take turns to be fed a fish, and never snatch their supper. This is different from the unpleasant display of shark table manners known as the "feeding frenzy". That's when sharks get over-excited at feeding time and end up biting each other in a bid to get more than their fair share of grisly grub.

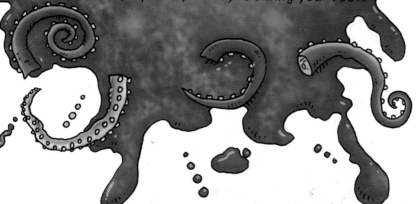

Bet you never knew!

There's a fearsome feeding frenzy to be seen off the Californian coast on moonless winter nights. Thousands of squid meet to mate and then die. Beastly blue sharks gatecrash the party and scoff all the squid they can, and then vomit them up so they can enjoy a second helping. Actually, shark-eating habits aren't nice at the best of times, especially if they're eating your foot...

SHARK-SPOTTERS' TRAINING TEST:
EAT LIKE A GREAT WHITE SHARK

You will need:
A set of shark jaws (if you don't happen to have any, you could use your own eating equipment).
Some tasty ham or a fish finger. In the interests of realism you really ought to practice on a wriggling fish, but this could be cruel to Bubbles.

What you do:
1 Raise your chin and jut your jaw forward.
2 Push forward your dagger-like lower teeth to stab your victim.
3 Thrust your upper jaw forward and down to slice your terrified prey from another direction.
4 Shake your head from side to side to rip off a giant chunk of flesh. Gulp it down without chewing.
5 Swim off, leaving your victim to die from loss of blood.

You should find:
Actually, you don't need to try step 5. Steps 1–4 are quite messy, and that's why sharks aren't welcome in posh restaurants. Since they don't have cheeks and can't chew, some of their food tends to float away.

HORRIBLE FAMILY WARNING
It isn't terribly clever to demonstrate your shark feeding skills to your family when the posh relatives come round for nibbles. You'll probably end up being fed fish food or fed to the fish.

Bet you never knew!
1 Great white sharks have a bone-crunching bite with a force of three tonnes per square centimetre. If you want to know what that feels like try balancing half an elephant on your little finger. Er, on second thoughts DON'T...
2 Grey nurse sharks feed by sucking fish into their massive mouths. I guess the sharks say "so long suckers" to their vanishing victims.

Hopefully you enjoyed your shark snack. Sharks generally do. If you want an instant idea of what a shark prefers to munch you need to take a close look at their teeth. Of course you might get your head bitten off...

SHARK-SPOTTERS' LESSON 7:
LOOKING AT SHARK TEETH

Here's a shark dentist's view of four types of shark jaws.

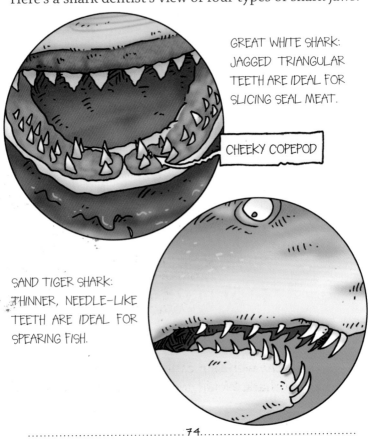

GREAT WHITE SHARK: JAGGED TRIANGULAR TEETH ARE IDEAL FOR SLICING SEAL MEAT.

CHEEKY COPEPOD

SAND TIGER SHARK: THINNER, NEEDLE-LIKE TEETH ARE IDEAL FOR SPEARING FISH.

TIGER SHARK:
TRIANGULAR TEETH, NARROWER THAN THE GREAT WHITE'S. CAN HANDLE JUST ABOUT ANYTHING - INCLUDING YOU.

GUMMY SHARK:
NO SHARP TEETH. FLAT PLATE-LIKE TEETH FOR CRUSHING PREY.

The prize for the world's most easily pleased feeder goes to ... the tiger shark. Would you fancy a tiger shark snack?

The Daily Shark

Restaurant Review
THE TIGER SHARK DINER

Important scientific note for tiger-shark spotters
I bet you think that I made this up – but _all_ these items have been found inside tiger sharks.

The diner was packed with happy tiger sharks – they were having a real feeding frenzy! As an appetiser I tried a car number plate, which was pleasantly crunchy although a little rusty at the edges. My shark mate tucked into a pair of human trousers but they were rather tasteless and disappointing as there was no human inside them.

There followed a mixed serving of dead seagulls, lumps of coal, paint cans and car parts served buffet-style with everyone helping themselves. Delicious – I certainly bit off more than I could chew!

Next week we'll be dropping into the Great White Restaurant to sample delicious dead dog served very rare with seaweed!

But talking about tiger sharks – by some ghastly coincidence, one has just turned up for dinner at Skull Island. Will a helping of Harvey prove too huge for the hungry shark?

Like most reefs, Skull Island reef is divided into territories where different sharks rule the waves.

1 Black-tip reef sharks swim into the shallow water. Careful where you paddle!

2 White-tip reef sharks lurk in deeper water (up to 40 metres) close to underwater cliffs.

3 Grey reef sharks live in zone 2, but prefer water deeper than 25 metres. They like to get an in-depth view.

4 Tiger sharks live in the open ocean but often pay a visit. It's a bit like you turning up at the local takeaway. This is bad news for the local sharks, as the tiger scrunches smaller sharks along with car number plates and people and everything else you can imagine.

All this goes to prove that although shark brains haven't grown in 450 million years, they're smart enough to avoid fights even though different species hunt similar prey. Grey reef sharks, the sort that Captain Snapper's been feeding, have a way to warn other sharks off their patch. Want to know what it is? Well, here's your chance to make all the right moves…

SHARK-SPOTTERS' TRAINING TEST
THE REEF SHARK THREAT DANCE

What you need:
Yourself
You might like to invite a good friend or Bubbles the goldfish to be part of your act, but this isn't essential.
Some cool music

What you do:
1 Switch the music on. Unlike the shark, you don't have to dance underwater. Just follow the moves as demonstrated by Harvey Tucker.

2 Get in position:

3 Walk towards your partner in an S-shaped path until you're 1 metre from them, then turn away. As you move, you should bob your head up and down. Walk back in another S-shape so that you've travelled in a figure of eight.

4 Repeat steps 2 and 3 until your partner backs off, or falls about laughing.

You should find:
You'll feel like a half-witted penguin, and to be honest, you really need to be a shark to look at all scary.

As luck would have it, the friendly reef sharks perform their dance and persuade the tiger shark that it's not welcome. Harvey returns to the ship feeling tired but happy. But just then the phone rings...

Has Harvey's luck run out even faster than his secret supply of biscuits? You'll have to dip into the next chapter to find out...

SCARY GREAT WHITE SHARKS

We'll leave Harvey panicking under his duvet and talk about something nicer – shark babies, for instance. Well, come to think of it, sharks aren't much known for their family life. In fact I'm surprised they don't have personal problems...

 MY FAMILY WANT TO EAT ME
An underwater play

A young great white shark is lying on a couch talking to a seal therapist.

ST: So when did your problems begin?

GWS: They started before I was born and I ate my brothers and sisters while we were still inside our mum. Some of them were babies and some were eggs.

ST: Veeeeery interesting! And did your brothers and sisters disagree with you?

GWS: Only after I ate them. I felt really poorly! I blame mum. Me and my brothers and sisters were feeding on egg yolk. Then the yolk ran out. It was no yolk when we got peckish...

ST: Did you have a guilty feeling?

GWS: It was more of a gill-tea feeding...

ST: Don't feel too bad. Many species of shark have live young and the babies feed off each other before birth.

GWS: After I was born my mum swam off and left me and my remaining brothers and sisters to roam alone.

ST: All shark mothers abandon their young. It's safer, adult sharks often eat shark babies. How did you survive?

GWS: I ate small fish and crabs. It helps having pointy teeth. But just recently my teeth have got triangular and I've developed a craving for meat...

ST: Er, I think we've just timed-out. That's to say, it's time I wasn't here.

GWS: Oh don't go – I'd LOVE to eat you, er, meat you. How about dinner?

Exit shark chasing seal therapist. Curtain falls and underwater audience boo and throw mouldy kippers at the author.

Meanwhile, back on Captain Snapper's boat, our intrepid shark-spotting heroes have arrived at Blood Reef, the well-known haunt of great white sharks*... but there are no great whites about. Well, what do you expect? Great whites don't turn up to order. So that means our heroes have to invite the sharks to dinner...

SHARK-SPOTTERS' LESSON 8:
HOW TO INVITE A GREAT WHITE SHARK TO DINNER

As a shark-spotter you need to know how to lure sharks to your neighbourhood. The good news is that big sharks are often attracted to boats – the underside of the boat looks like a dead whale, and the electric currents from any metal in the hull are another draw.

To encourage the great whites to get up close and personal you need to give them something nice to sniff. So you dangle mouldy tuna fish and dump vast amounts of stinky chum into the sea.

"A vast stinky chum?" I hear you mumble. Am I talking about our outsized pal Harvey Tucker? No, I'm not!

OI!

*Don't waste time with the atlas – this is another made-up place.

Captain Red Snapper's Patent Chum Mixture

(or Berley as we Aussies call it)

Ingredients:
Rotting fish heads
Fish guts and other unmentionable bits that the cat won't touch.
Rotting horse meat (sharks love it!)
Blood
Clothes peg

Method:
1 Put clothes peg on nose.
2 Mix up all the other ingredients and spend days tipping them over the side.

The sharks will turn up soon, and Harvey's in a panic. The Captain wants him to dive in a cage hung from the boat. The problem is the chum has told the shark it's dinnertime, and now there's a tasty human in an outfit that makes him look a bit like a seal, in a cage which gives out tempting electrical signals. What shark wouldn't feel hungry?

So what can Harvey do?

SHARK-SPOTTERS' LESSON 9:
HOW TO PROTECT YOURSELF FROM GETTING SCRUNCHED BY A SHARK

Let's start off with some methods that we definitely don't recommend to shark-spotters. Well, not unless you actually *want* to get chomped...

1 Shipwrecked sailors in the Second World War were told to kick and splash to scare off sharks.

Verdict: More likely to summon sharks. Modern experts suggest crouching in the water or huddling in a group and trying not to move.

2 Worship the shark as a god – if you make friends with them, they'll protect you. You could even kill a pig and spill its blood in the sea and share the meat with your new bloodthirsty buddies.

Verdict: That's what Solomon Islanders do, although shark worship was common amongst many Pacific peoples. Personally speaking, I wouldn't share my bacon butty with a snatching shark.

3 Tattoo your ankles like some Hawaiian women.

Verdict: It won't work so why "foot" the bill?

4 Wear a long strip of red cloth attached to your traditional underwater wear (as worn by Japanese lady abalone divers). The sharks bite the red cloth rather than your backside.

Verdict: No diver wearing the cloth has ever been bitten. But no one's been attacked without it either.

As I said at the start, none of these methods work – but to be honest, many modern methods aren't much better. Which of these anti-shark devices actually works and which is as useful as a concrete trampoline?

SHARK-SPOTTERS' TRAINING TEST:
PICK A PROVEN PROTECTOR

1 Put up nets – that'll keep the sharks out.

2 Hide in a giant plastic bag with a floating rim that looks like a paddling pool. The sharks won't know you're inside.

3 Disguise yourself as a pilot fish – wear a black and white stripy wetsuit.

4 Wear armour made of thousands of metal links. Sharks can't use can openers so you should be safe.

5 Take refuge behind a screen of bubbles. The sharks will be scared off.

6 Squirt a nasty chemical at the sharks. They'll soon lose their taste for you.

7 Carry a weapon such as a long stick, a spear gun with an exploding head, an electric shock prod, etc. The sharks won't dare mess with you when they see how hard you are.

Answers:

Proper protection

1 Nets protect some beaches in South Africa and Australia. Trouble is, they kill lots of sharks plus innocent dolphins and turtles.

2 The bag seems to work – just so long as you don't mind looking like a giant jellyfish.

4 The armour protects its wearer from a nip by a small shark. But a great white will crush the human and the armour is very expensive. What's more, the metal tends to attract sharks at awkward moments.

6 Only some chemicals work – so you can have half a point. In the Second World War, the US Navy tried a substance called "shark chaser", but later tests showed it was as useless as a dinosaur in a spelling contest. The shampoo ingredient sodium lauryl sulphate does work. Sharks think it tastes almost as vile as Brussels sprout flavoured ice cream.

7 The weapons work if you want to kill the shark, but true shark-spotters want to study sharks and not bump them off.

Fishy failures

3 Sharks sometimes eat pilot fish. They might sometimes eat you too.

5 The bubbles fence was the work of an Australian inventor in 1960, but the plan popped even faster than the bubbles.

Back on Captain Snapper's boat, the dreaded hour strikes for Harvey Tucker. A great white is circling the vessel, and it's time for Harvey to take his place in the cage. It's unfortunate that Harvey's still clutching his bag of fishy-snacks – and it's even more unlucky that great whites love fishy-snacks too. Oh well – time for some typical great white attack behaviour...

First the shark circles the cage. Then it bumps it ... and then it attacks suddenly from behind and below, where Harvey can't see it. Its eyes roll back for protection as it opens its giant jaws... Is Harvey fish food?

HARVEY TUCKER IN ... FISHY FLOP FURY

Is it all over for Harvey? Is he about to meet a finny finale at the moment of tooth – er, truth? The next page will reveal all!

EPILOGUE: SAVAGE SHARKS?

Few things are ever as bad as they seem. After sinking the boat, the shark is left in shock. And it leaves in a hurry after the fishy-snacks give it an upset tummy ... allowing the humans to swim to safety.

The photo looks fantastic and the editor is all smiles – until she gets the bill for the boat. Hmm ... it looks like Harvey's article is all about how savage sharks are – but is it just an ugly rumour?

Bet you never knew!
In the 1960s, Australian scientists tried to find out which words upset people most. And the scariest word – more terrifying than "murder", "poison", or "spider" – proved to be "SHARK"!

Maybe sharks scare us humans because we can't control them, and once we're in the water, we're at their mercy. But then we're catching them like there's no tomorrow – which for the sharks there probably isn't. Many sharks don't produce young until they're five or more years old, so there's no way they can make up their numbers.

In 2009, scientists announced that out of 21 species of open ocean shark no fewer than 16 were heading for extinction. Extinction – that means died out. It means no more biting people, because there won't be any sharks to do the biting. Not now and not ever. Of course it would make the world a teeny bit safer for humans, but wouldn't it make the world more boring too?

As a fully fledged shark-spotter, I'm sure you know the answer!

Answer, page 64: the deadly blue-ringed octopus is lurking at the bottom of page 81.

HORRIBLE INDEX